The Every Kid Club

by Anne O'Brien
illustrated by Gioia Fiammenghi

Practice Decodable 87

McGraw Hill Education

Bothell, WA • Chicago, IL • Columbus, OH • New York, NY

MHEonline.com

Send all inquiries to:
McGraw-Hill Education
8787 Orion Place
Columbus, OH 43240

ISBN: 978-0-02-138080-0
MHID: 0-02-138080-5

Printed in China.

8 9 10 11 12 DSS 27 26 25 24 23

Abby and Rose went over to Nancy's yard to play.

"Hurry up!" called Nancy.
"We can play in my tree house!"

"Wow! What a neat place!" said Abby.
"Let's make a club!" said Rose.
"We can call it the Three Girls Club."

Rose got out paints and paper.

Abby painted THREE GIRLS CLUB and three faces on the paper.

"Hi!" called Holly. "Can I climb up?"

Nancy said, "We have a club. It's called the Three Girls Club. You would make four."

Holly looked down. She hung her head.

"Well," said Nancy, "how about just Girls Club?"
Abby crossed out THREE and painted a face.
"Now we are the Girls Club!" shouted Rose.

"Hi!" called David. "Can I climb up?"

"Well," said Nancy, "this is a club for girls, and you aren't a girl."

David frowned. He kicked the dirt.

"Well," said Nancy, "how about the First Grade Club?"

Abby crossed out GIRLS and painted FIRST GRADE.

Then she painted a fifth face.

"Now we are the First Grade Club!" said Rose.

"Hi!" called Nancy's big brother, Tom. "Can I climb up?"

"Well," said Nancy, "this is the First Grade Club, and you aren't in first grade."

Tom scowled.

"Well," said Holly, "how about the All Grades Club?"

Abby crossed out FIRST, added an S, and painted ALL.

Then she painted a sixth face.

"Now we are the All Grades Club!" chuckled Rose.

"Hi!" called Abby's little sister.

"Can I come up?"

"Well," said Abby, "we have a club. It's called the All Grades Club, and you aren't even in kindergarten!"

"It's getting crowded!" said Rose. "How about just calling it the Every Kid Club?"

Abby crossed out ALL GRADES and painted EVERY KID. Then she painted lots of faces.

"The Every Kid Club is lots of fun!" shouted Rose.